BUNCHGRASS and
BUTTERCUPS

BUNCHGRASS and BUTTERCUPS

FINNISH-AMERICAN POEMS and PROSE

Kiitos!

GARY V. ANDERSON

Gary V. Ander—

Cover Photo: L. Lotus, Vashon Island, Washington
                     Buttercups

Author Photo: Roberta Lang

ISBN 978-0-615-61901-9

Printed in the United States of America
SHELTER BAY PUBLISHING
Bainbridge Island, Washington

For my grandsons,
Tyler, Arik and Deven

Boys, others will tell you of an old logging town
named Deep River. But I want you to search for a
40 acre farm up the road—Grandpa's Deep River.
What I have written in this book will give you
a glimpse of the life we lived there.

Here are the directions:

East of Long Beach,
west of Longview,
east of Naselle,
west of Grays River,
east of Salme Hill,
west of Seal River,
east of Hedlund,
west of Nikkila,
east of Bakkila,
west of Wirkkala.

Latitude 46° 21' 1.86" North
Longitude 123° 40' 56.81" West

Contents

I. THE DEEP RIVER SUITE

The first stanza of this poem describes a well-known Finnish value. The second stanza, a representation of my childhood Finnish experience—a self portrait.

Deep River Finn

Nature is solitude,
not meant for entertainment.
You stay home, friend,

leave me to my longing.

At sunrise
in the Willapa Hills,
the robin begins,
solo, A cappella.

Deep River Suomalainen

Luonto on yksinäisyys,
eikä tarkoitettu viihdyttämään.
Pysy kotona, ystävä,

jätä minut ikävöimään.

Auringonnousussa
Willapan Kukkuloilla,
punarintarastas aloittaa,
soolon, ilman säestystä.

3

It is not often you land in soft grass and flowers—
not in life and not on the farm.

One of Those Days

Sit
on a cow,
push the barn door open
with one foot,
nothing to grasp—hope
to make it through
barn yard muck—
to land softly in
bunchgrass
and
buttercups.

But then,
little goes right
down on the farm.

Of all the liars in the world sometimes the worst are your own fears.
—Rudyard Kipling

Old Growth

I follow a trail
down the ridge
in fading light;
nothing but
open space
under these hemlocks.

I remember Grandpa's
story about crossing
on this path,
Seal River to
Deep River
in the moonlight;
how he returned at dawn,
finding cougar tracks,
in his boot prints.

I stop,
feel an adrenaline rush.
Quill-hairs rise
on the back of my neck.

I clap my hands,
rattle the backpack,
sing a hiking song.

Nothing but space—
even I know that.

I have been in plenty of embarrassing situations in my adult life. The best I can do is go back to this character builder and laugh it off.

Fifteen cows

morning and night.

Contemplate
the line of
swayback Jerseys,
listen to the
steady rhythm of
the Surge milking machine;
think about the
dry manure
behind your ear
discovered after school.

We had a personal relationship with our food—we ate our pets. So did you, if you were in 4-H or FFA!

Bruce

lowered his head
to sniff his last
handful of grain.
The gunman
just inside
the barn door
earned half a liver
for the thirty ought six
clean shot
between the eyes.

Bled,
skinned,
gutted,
aged seven days,
hacked into pieces on
the kitchen table.

Friend, Bruce,
raised from a calf,
castrated, grass fed,
organic.

The day might have gone better if we had stolen the home brew and left the canned blackberries.

All We Wanted Was PB & J

Nothin' in the
fridge but
an ancient box of
Arm & Hammer and three
bottles of the old man's
home brew.

Gather the brothers.
Climb up to the
vine maple grove,
with one jar of
canned blackberries
taken from the cellar.

While we were gone,
missed little sister's
first sentence,
Aw shit, no bread.
We got a whippin'
for that.

Just some of the many unanswered questions.

So Much

Why does it
take so much
milk
to make
cheese?

So much
sap
to make
maple syrup?

And so much
love
to overcome
one hateful
word?

I am a sucker for girls with accordions, short skirts, and mesh stockings.

Tanssia
Finnish for The Dance

I drop a few bills
into the
accordion case
and ask for a tune
in A minor.
She says *ok.*
I ask if she's
from Finland.
She says, *no, Astoria,*
but I can play in A minor.

I see sweet
Finn girls
across the
Tango hall,
hear one-two-three,
stomp of schottische,
taste cinnamon
korvapuusti
warm from the oven.

I open my eyes.

She asks,
Can you feel A minor?
Yes, I whisper, *yes.*

There is a Sami word, mahkalahke. It means to return to a place you once lived in order to find something you've lost.

In my twenties, I asked my mother what kind of a boy I was. She said, "You were moody." Like many writers, I do not know what some of my poems are about, or where they come from. I think this one might be about childhood depression.

Onkalo
Finnish for hiding place

Return to a place
once lived,
find something
once lost.

Hold undamaged
parts of soul and self
as dew settles
on lowlands.

Find the cedar stump,
burned hollow,
pull the sword fern
door closed,
dig for childish artifacts
buried there.

Touch flat rocks
from fast water,
say *skyfixer,*
say *dreamstream.*

Cry,
finally cry,
for the boy.

This is as clear as I can be on my value for the land. I would like to thank the foresters and conservationists in my life: Russ, Kent, Tina, and Helen. Bless you for the work you have done.

Dividing the Farm

You take fences,
tilled fields,
straight lines,
square corners
of forty.
Give me
meander of
stream, bank of
cattails, willow.

You take tree farm,
clear cut.
Give me
tangle of swamp,
knoll above marsh where
salt meets fresh,
vernal pond where
salamanders arrive
one spring night from
down under woody debris.

II. WILLAPA HILLS LOGGERS

The last line in this poem is from my Dad's oft-repeated story. The dynamite is from personal experience!

Rookie Logger Instruction Set–1

*Push the choker
under the log. We have'ta
get the choker around the log
to pull it to the landing.
Can't get'er
under the log?
Don't worry,
Put a stick of this powder
in the hole.*

*Everybody—
on the log,*
The riggin' slinger shouted,
*Did you push the firing cap
into the dynamite?
Good. When I touch
these wires to the battery—
jump.*

Wasn't that fun, boys?

*Charlie, you didn't jump!
I saw your false teeth
flyin' by. Get down
there and tell me
what you see.*

Toothless Charlie replied,
*Nothin' in 'der but
'labs, 'livers and 'ruce limbs.*

The first day on the job is always the scariest.

Rookie Logger Instruction Set–2

On your first day of loggin',
don't wear the brand
spankin' new
bright orange-glow rain
suit, the never worn
WHITE-OX gloves, fresh
oiled cork shoes, or the
never-used yellow
tin hat.

Sunday evening, after
supper, throw those
items in the nearest
mud hole,
run over 'em with
your pickup truck—
makes your first day
go better.

Loggers I knew had unusual ways of showing affection for their fathers.

Pentti's Bar

I hated my old man.
He made us pull
tumbleweed, and clear lots
for all those houses
he built in Arizona.
We were just kids.

As I finished my beer
a young logger in a hickory shirt
leaned close to his buddy
and said,

Every one of those houses
was thirty by forty.
Do you remember the
Py-thag-orean Theorem?
The diagonal had to be
exactly fifty.
Remember $a^2 + b^2 = c^2$?
Do you know what happens
when you get a foundation square?
It's like magic.
The siding goes on better,
the drywall and the cabinets fit.
The whole house goes up faster.

I hated that sonofabitch

III. TOO MUCH END TIME

Rose bushes and ashes just don't stay put.

Pink Rose

I search through
blackberry brambles,
alder saplings,
slip on wet clay,
where the
old house stood.

I hope to
find you, Mom,
wonder where
your climbing
pink rose
has gone.

Ashes are overrated,
I yearn for stone.

In Buddhism one is taught to meditate by riding the breath into the inner life, to the habitat of the soul.
—From Bill Moyers' conversation with Robert Hass, *The Language of Life, A Festival of Poets*

Invitation

When I am gone,
you might read
these poems,
take my lead,
ride
my breath
into my soul,
hear my heart,
breathe
with me.

It's a blessing when bad memories pack their bags—
not so, when good memories decide to go with them.
It's no vacation—they are not coming back.

Trilogy in Four Parts

Three songs,
three photographs,
three places to look for a lost life.

The Playlist
    All from Pink Floyd–The Wall–side 2:

> *Nobody Home*
> *Comfortably Numb*
> *Is There Anybody Out There?*

> *Is there anybody in there?*

The Photographs
    A man and a woman.
    A young couple and a boy.
    A house on a lake.

> *Who's this?*
> *Who's this?*
> *Where did you take this one?*

And again, as if new

> *Who's this?*
> *Who's this?*
> *Where did you take this one?*

The Visit
    When there is nothing left to say,
    the silence unbearable,
    I ask,
    do you watch television?

You answer, *yes.*
There, and there, and there.

You know you are lost when your work begins to talk back to you.

Poem's Complaint

He thinks
he writes
me. We
both know
I write him.
It feels
good to be
shaped, tweaked,
edited;
like a massage
or haircut.

Sometimes,
he leaves
me feeling
naked, removes
most of my
words, leaves me
wanting.

*When the Greeks imagined Gods in their image,
who could have known Man would become the
center of the universe—take the earth as his own
and claim dominion over every living thing?*

First ice

at first light.
It's the last Sunday
morning on Deer Lake.

Eagle
on the ice—
eye level,
watching the struggle,
stares at the
splayed deer.
Together they wait for
coyote and wolf.

As he watches
from a distance
he thinks,
    if only you could
    survive the day—
    get up.
    Get your legs
    under you.
    Gather yourself.
    Be a trophy buck.
    I only take the very best,
    the finest specimen
    for my wall.

IV. WAR STORIES

I often wonder if the parents of this dead soldier were ever told he was killed over a gambling debt.

Guard Duty

I replace
the guy
killed here last night.
One shot
between the eyes,
close range,
with a .45,
like the one
on my hip.

Sgt Maki said,
Your duty tonight is
the motor pool.
Don't stand in one place,
walk around.
You see the enemy,
shoot 'im.

Alone,
I side-step shadows,
avoid empty trucks,
tail gates up,
canvas flapping in wind.

Who is the enemy?
What does he look like?

I hear a shot.

Reflex takes me
to the ground,
safety off.
I feel warm piss,
listen to the
generator regain its
composure.

I spend the next year
learning to value shadows,
hiding in them,
searching for light
that makes them possible.

Flashback

*If grandmothers and children were in charge of the world,
there would never be any wars.*
—Naomi Shihab Nye, *19 Varieties of Gazelle*

I go back to 1968, to the barracks in Nha Trang,
where I'm snapping a picture of six young Vietnamese
women, girls actually, all hiding their faces with *nón lá,*
leaf hats, except one. She looked directly at me. Days
after that picture was taken we decided on a date and
time as she handed me her address. Well, I thought, I
just got lucky!

On the appointed day, I went into the village and
knocked on her door. She ushered me through an
empty room into a second room with a wooden bed
covered in bamboo matting. The girl motioned for me
to lie down, while she positioned a small pillow under
my head. At that moment, I realized she wanted me to
nap. I dozed among rustling noises from the next room.

When I awoke, I could smell food. Again she took my
hand and led me back into the first room. There, in the
middle of the floor, was a small cook pot with rice, one
filet of white fish and chopsticks.

There were three pillows.
One for me,
one for her,
one for her
elderly grandmother.

We ate that sparse banquet in silence. She led me to the
door, hugged me and nudged me out into the war from
which I had come.

Forget the thanks, I'll take an apology

It is no secret that "support our troops" was coined by hawks who hoped to blackmail Americans into abandoning the call for answerability for sacrificing those very troops to a questionable war. It strikes me that the vociferous demand for government accountability from that quarter of the political spectrum doesn't seem to reach to a call for proving that the crippling billions that are poured into foreign warfare are not more about politics and commerce than national defense.

As a veteran of our intrusion into Vietnam that never posed a moment's threat to my country, I feel less deserving of thanks or gratitude than an apology for squandering the lives of my comrades in these shameless exercises in international bullying and possibly even trading their lives for capital gain. Before you ask us to kill and die in your name, you should protect that name by demanding we be absolutely sure we really should.

—An excerpt from a guest editorial
Nov 14, 2010, *Seattle Times*
Harold R. Pettus, Everett, Washington

After the War

He held a
cardboard sign,
Vet—
anything will help,
whispered,
I think about the war
every day,
suicide not as often.

V. RECIPES

This was a large part of our diet in Deep River.

Laksloda

A dozen Yukon Gold or Yellow Finn potatoes
washed and sliced (no need to peel)

2 cups of smoked salmon*

1 large yellow onion, chopped

½ cup milk or cream

salt and pepper to taste

Heat oven to 350 degrees. Butter a large covered
casserole. Layer the salmon, potatoes and onions
Add the milk or cream, salt, and pepper. Cover the
casserole. Bake for about an hour or until the potatoes
are done.

* The best salmon for Laksloda is suolakala, or salt fish.
The best recipe for suolakala was recorded by Harte
Pentilla and can be found on page 57 of *My Finnish
Soul,* or *The Country Cousins' Cookbook,* Anderson-
Matta-Owens Family Reunion, August 15, 1987.

A modern recipe crafted by Steve Ullakko. You can see his demonstration and get his advice on this delicacy at the Finnish–American Folk Festival, Naselle, Washington.

Korvapuusti in a Bread Machine

1 egg

1 cup milk (2.5 dl*)

3 cups flour (7 dl)

½ cup sugar (1 dl)

½ tsp salt

1 tsp cardamom

3 ½ tsp dry yeast

6 tbsp butter (melted but not hot)

cinnamon and vanilla sugar mix

sugar crystals

First put egg and milk in bread machine, then add flour, sugar, salt, cardamom and yeast on top of other dry ingredients. Add melted butter just as you start machine. Let machine do first rise of dough.

Roll out dough and spread with butter, sugar, cinnamon, and vanilla sugar mix. Roll up and cut at angles /\/\/\. Push down on top of triangle to push out sides. Let raise until double their size. Brush with beaten egg and sprinkle with sugar crystals.

Bake at 350 degrees for 8–12 minutes. Watch closely for lighter color on top.

dl is deciliter, a metric measure of volume used in Finland.

This recipe is from my son, Justin Anderson, and passed down from his maternal grandmother, Dorothy Johnson Anderson.

Never Fail Sweet Rye Bread

COMBINE:

⅔ cup molasses

⅔ cup white Karo syrup

1 cup brown sugar

4 cups milk

4 tbsp fat

Scald (heat) the above ingredients and cool

ADD:

4 cups rye flour

2 tbsp salt

3 pkgs. yeast, dissolved in 1 cup warm water
(Grandma doesn't use the fast rising kind.)

To this mixture add about 12 cups white flour to
make a stiff dough. Place in bowl and cover with
cloth. Let rise until double in bulk. (When you poke
a finger in the dough and the indentation stays, it is
ready. Takes about 3 hours.) Knead 100 times, using
as little flour as possible.

Shape into loaves and place in greased pans. Let rise
until double in bulk (use finger test again). Bake at
425 degrees for 15 minutes, then reduce heat to 325
degrees and bake 35 minutes more. May have to cover
top with foil so it doesn't get too brown.

Acknowledgements

"Deep River Finn," "So Much," "Fifteen Cows," and "Tanssia" were previously published in *Kippis! A Literary Journal of the Finnish North American Literature Association.*

"One of Those Days" and "Old Growth" were published in *Curio Poetry,* New York.

"Deep River Finn" was translated to the Finnish language by Sirpa Kaukinen.

Thanks to John, David S., Marit, Neil, David H., and Kris, mentors at the Strawberry Hill Poetry Workshop, for continued guidance and support. Also, thanks to Sheila Bender at Writing it Real for her valuable writing prompts and encouragement.

Thanks to Jani Kattilakoski, Mikkeli, Finland for his help with the Finnish language.

This poetry book was typeset and edited by Sue Cook Visuals, Seattle, Washington.

Thanks especially to Roberta Lang for sustenance, in all its forms.

Author

Gary V. Anderson, Pacific Northwest Folk Poet, has been the moderator for spoken word events at Finnish American Folk Festivals in Naselle, Washington, and FinnFest USA in Astoria, Oregon.

He writes about growing up Finn, man's relationship with the natural environment, and ironies when looking back over more than sixty years.

This is Gary's second book of poems and prose. The first, *My Finnish Soul,* was published in 2010.

Order Form

To order
BUNCHGRASS and BUTTERCUPS

or the author's first book
MY FINNISH SOUL:

Please send a check or money order
for $15.00 per book (or $25 for both) to:

GARY V. ANDERSON
713 Madison Ave. N.
Bainbridge Island, Washington 98110

Includes shipping and handling.

Or go to:
www.garyandersonpoetry.com

Made in the USA
San Bernardino, CA
06 September 2017